ZOOM IN ON
GRASSHOPPERS

ZOOM
In on
Insects!

Melissa Stewart

CONTENTS

WORDS TO KNOW

antennae (an TEN ee)—Two long, thin body parts on the head of insects and some other animals. Antennae help animals sense the world around them.

nymph (NIMF)—The second part in the life cycle of some insects. A nymph changes into an adult.

GRASSHOPPER HOMES

ZOOM BUBBLE

Grasshoppers live in many parts of the world. They need warm weather and lots of plants to eat.

You'll find some kinds of grasshoppers in fields, gardens, and deserts. Others live in trees and bushes.

PARTS OF A GRASSHOPPER

antennae

head

eye

wing

leg

abdomen

thorax

GRASSHOPPER BODY

ZOOM BUBBLE

A grasshopper is an insect. An insect has six legs. And its body has three parts.

An insect's head is in the front. The thorax is in the middle. The abdomen is the part at the back.

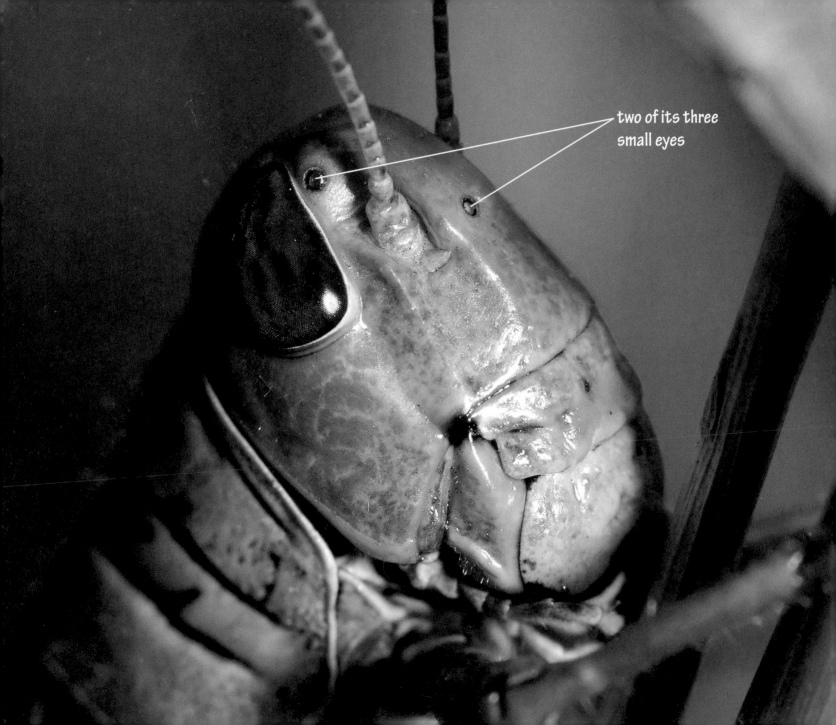

two of its three
small eyes

GRASSHOPPER EYES

ZOOM BUBBLE

See the two big eyes on this grasshopper's head? They help it see shapes and colors. They can tell when something moves.

A grasshopper also has three small eyes. They can tell if it is day or night.

GRASSHOPPER ANTENNAE

ZOOM BUBBLE

A grasshopper has two long antennae on the top of its head. They can feel and smell. Some can hear, too. But most grasshoppers have ears on their legs!

GRASSHOPPER LEGS

A grasshopper has six legs. They are attached to the middle of its body.

A grasshopper uses its legs to walk from place to place. The front legs can hold food. The back legs help the insect jump through the air.

GRASSHOPPER WINGS

ZOOM BUBBLE

Most grasshoppers have two sets of wings. But they do not fly as well as other insects. Grasshoppers stretch out their wings when they jump. That helps them glide a long way.

GRASSHOPPER FOOD

ZOOM BUBBLE

A grasshopper is not a picky eater. It will munch on any plant it can find. It likes the grass in your yard. It likes corn, wheat, and clover, too. It even eats tree bark.

GRASSHOPPER COLOR

ZOOM BUBBLE

Many grasshoppers are green. They stay safe by blending in with leaves.

Other grasshoppers eat plants that are full of poison. Then they become poisonous, too. Their bright bodies send out a message. They say, "Don't eat me. You will get sick."

This nymph does not have wings.

GRASSHOPPER NYMPHS

ZOOM BUBBLE

A young grasshopper is called a **nymph**. It looks a lot like its parents. But it is small and has no wings.

The nymph eats and grows, eats and grows. After six to eight weeks, it turns into an adult.

LIFE CYCLE

A grasshopper starts its life inside an EGG.

A NYMPH eats twice its weight in food every day.

An ADULT grasshopper dies at the end of summer.

LEARN MORE

BOOKS

Ashley, Susan. *Incredible Grasshoppers*. New York: Gareth Stevens, 2011.

Nelson, Robin. *Grasshoppers*. Minneapolis: Lerner, 2009.

Silverman, Buffy. *Can You Tell a Cricket From a Grasshopper?*
   Minneapolis: Lerner, 2012.

WEB SITES

Grasshopper Facts for Kids
   <http://animalstime.com/grasshopper-facts-kids-grasshopper-diet-habitat>

Live Science: Insects
   <http://www.livescience.com/topics/insect>

INDEX

Enslow Elementary, an imprint of Enslow Publishers, Inc.
Enslow Elementary® is a registered trademark of Enslow Publishers, Inc.

Copyright © 2014 by Melissa Stewart

Library of Congress Cataloging-in-Publication Data

Stewart, Melissa.
Zoom in on grasshoppers / Melissa Stewart.
p. cm. — (Zoom in on insects)
Summary: "Provides information for readers about a grasshopper's home, food, and body"—Provided by publisher.
Includes index.
ISBN 978-0-7660-4214-8
1. Grasshoppers—Juvenile literature. I. Title. II. Series: Stewart, Melissa. Zoom in on insects.
QL508.A2S85 2014
595.726—dc23
2012040391

Future editions:
Paperback ISBN: 978-1-4644-0371-2
EPUB ISBN: 978-1-4645-1205-6
Single-User ISBN: 978-1-4646-1205-3
Multi-User ISBN: 978-0-7660-5837-8

Printed in the United States of America
102013 Lake Book Manufacturing, Inc. Melrose Park, IL
10 9 8 7 6 5 4 3 2 1

To Our Readers: We have done our best to make sure all Internet Addresses in this book were active and appropriate when we went to press. However, the author and the publisher have no control over and assume no liability for the material available on those Internet sites or on other Web sites they may link to. Any comments or suggestions can be sent by e-mail to comments@enslow.com or to the address on the back cover.

♻ Enslow Publishers, Inc., is committed to printing our books on recycled paper. The paper in every book contains 10% to 30% post-consumer waste (PCW). The cover board on the outside of each book contains 100% PCW. Our goal is to do our part to help young people and the environment too!

Photo Credits: Andrea GonAalves/Photos.com, pp. 6, 22 (adult); Boris Pamikov/Photos.com, p. 17; David Acosta Allely/Photos.com, p. 21; © Dietmar Nill/NPL/Minden Pictures, p. 15; loraks/Photos.com, p. 5; © Murray, Patti/Animals Animals, p. 20; Richard Leighton/Photos.com, p. 18; Shutterstock.com, pp. 2, 3, 4, 7, 8, 9, 10, 11, 13, 16, 19, 22 (egg, nymph); © Stephen Dalton/Minden Pictures, p. 12, 14.

Cover Photo: Shutterstock.com

Enslow Elementary
an imprint of
Enslow Publishers, Inc.
40 Industrial Road
Box 398
Berkeley Heights, NJ 07922
USA
http://www.enslow.com

Series Literacy Consultant:
Allan A. De Fina, PhD
Dean, College of Education
New Jersey City University
Jersey City, New Jersey
Past President of the New Jersey Reading Association

Science Consultant:
Helen Hess, PhD
Professor of Biology
College of the Atlantic
Bar Harbor, Maine